A Tribute to
THE YOUNG AT HEART

E. B. WHITE

By Julie Berg

Published by Abdo & Daughters, 4940 Viking Drive, Suite 622, Edina, Minnesota 55435.

Library bound edition distributed by Rockbottom Books, Pentagon Tower, P.O. Box 36036, Minneapolis, Minnesota 55435.

Printed in the United States.

Cover Photo credit: Bettmann Archives
Interior Photo credits Bettmann Archives, pages 5, 13, 26
Wide World, page 23, 31

Edited by Rosemary Wallner

Library of Congress Cataloging-in-Publication Data

Berg, Julie.
    E.B. White / Julie Berg.
       p.   cm. -- (A Tribute to the Young at Heart)
    ISBN 1-56239-356-1   ISBN 1-56239-367-7 (prbk..)
    1. White, E.B. (Elwyn Brooks), 1899--Juvenile literature.
    2. Authors, American--20th century--Biography--Juvenile
    literature. 3. Children's stories--Authorship--Juvenile
    literature. [1. White, E.B. (Elwyn Brooks), 1899-- .
    2. Authors, American.] I. Title. II. Series.
    PS3545.H5187Z527   1994
    818'.5209--dc20   94-5307
    [B]   CIP
                                            AC

TABLE OF CONTENTS

A CLASSIC WRITER

E. B. White was an essayist, poet, and humorist for adults. Though he died in 1985, he is still recognized as one of the world's foremost prose writers. During his long and successful writing career, White also authored three stories for middle graders, *Stuart Little* (1945), *Charlotte's Web* (1952), and *The Trumpet of the Swan* (1970).

In these books, White blended fantasy and realism to present important ideas to young readers. He used narratives that reflected his personal philosophy and style. All three books were commercial successes. But *Charlotte's Web* was considered not only White's best book for children, but also the crowning achievement of his career. Today, the book is still praised as the classic American children's book of the twentieth century.

E.B. White was awarded a gold medal for essays by the
National Institute of Arts and Letters.

A MUSICAL CHILDHOOD

Elwyn Brooks (E. B.) White was born in Mount Vernon, New York, on July 11, 1899. He grew up in a comfortable home with his brothers, Marion, Albert, and Stanley, and his sisters, Clara and Lillian. White recalled spending "countless hours hobnobbing with James Bridges, the coachman, watching him polish harnesses and wash carriages."

White's father, Samuel Tilly White, worked for a piano company. He supplied his six children with a variety of musical instruments: a grand piano, a reed organ, violins, cellos, mandolins, guitars, banjos, and drums. Music filled the White household. White played the piano, picked at the mandolin, and took cello lessons. But he never developed musical talent and eventually gave up serious musical pursuits.

In 1904, five-year-old White entered kindergarten. He fought his parents with every ounce of strength. He wanted to stay home and live peacefully in familiar surroundings. The idea of school terrified him.

White spent the next nine years in P.S. 2. He rode his bicycle or walked to school. There were no school buses. School rules were strict. White's teachers did not tolerate any nonsense in the classrooms. White was a good student. His fear of falling behind inspired him to get good marks.

In 1913, White, now fourteen years old, went on to the Mount Vernon High School. He enjoyed Latin but never was able to master it. Being skinny and small, he didn't care for athletics. But he liked ice skating. On winter afternoons and evenings, he would visit a local pond and skate with his friends.

White graduated from high school in 1917. He won two scholarships totaling $1,000. He decided to attend Cornell University in Ithica, New York.

A WRITING CAREER BEGINS

While taking classes, White worked on the *Cornell Daily Sun*. At the end of his junior year, he was elected editor-in-chief. He became president of his fraternity and was elected to the senior honorary society, Quill and Dagger.

"I majored in English partly because I didn't know what else to do," White admitted. "But mostly because I did have a strong tendency to write."

Following graduation from Cornell in 1921, White went to New York City to find work. He took a job with the United Press—an organization similar to and rivaling the Associated Press.

"I started [writing] in the New York bureau Saturday morning," he recalled. "I could have had a job with the N.Y. Edison Company editing their (newspaper), if I had wanted to. I was seriously tempted, too. But my conscience troubled me. It was almost too soft—all I would have had to do would have been to sit in a beautifully upholstered private office with a stenographer who reads the *Saturday Evening Post* all day, and edit a small paper once a week."

In December 1921 White left the United Press and worked briefly for a public relations firm. By January 1922 he joined the American Legion News Service. The job gave White the opportunity to learn publicity. The articles he wrote reached 15,000 papers across the country.

SEATTLE AND ALASKA

In the spring of 1922, White quit his job and traveled across the United States with a friend. The two ended up in Seattle. In Seattle, White was a reporter for the *Seattle Times*. He worked from 7:30 a.m. until he completed his work—which was anywhere from 2:30 to 11:30 p.m., according to what his assignments had been.

When the *Seattle Times* laid him off in 1923, White boarded a ship, the *S.S. Buford*, bound for Alaska and Siberia. "My trip to Alaska, like practically everything else that happened to me in those busy years, was pure accident," he remembered. "I was living in Seattle; I was unemployed, my job on a newspaper having blown up in mid-June; and although I had no reason for going to Alaska, I had no reason for staying away, either."

White got a job on the ship. He worked from eight in the evening till six in the morning. He set tables, prepared late supper for thirty, served it, cleaned the tables, washed the dishes, swept down the companionway leading to the social hall, and shined brass.

By his own admittance, this was hard, dull work. At three o'clock in the morning, White would step out onto the forward deck for a break.

"With the sky showing bright in the north," he said, "and the mate pacing the bridge and the throaty snores of the passengers issuing from the staterooms, the ship would throb and tremble under me and she was my ship, all mine and right on course, alive and purposeful and exciting."

On September 4, the ship docked back in Seattle. White collected his pay, went ashore— and returned to his parents' home in Mount Vernon. Back in New York, he worked in the advertising business for the next two years.

THE NEW YORKER

In November 1925 twenty-six-year-old White moved to Manhattan, New York. "Everything was great, everything was exciting, except that for much of the time I didn't have a job, having drifted out of advertising, which I hated," he said. "I acquired a caged bird to keep me company." White tried freelancing. He also submitted poems and sketches to newspapers and magazines.

E.B. White writing for the *New Yorker* magazine in 1954.

Then Harold Ross's *New Yorker* arrived on the literary scene. This magazine was the turning point in White's life, although he did not know that at the time. He bought a copy of the first issue at a newsstand in Grand Central Station. He was attracted to the magazine, he said, "not because it had any great merit but because the items were short, relaxed, and sometimes funny."

White considered himself a short story writer. He lost no time submitting stories and poems to the new magazine. In return, he received a few small checks and the satisfaction of seeing his name in print as a professional writer.

In January 1927 White agreed to work part-time for the *New Yorker.* He gradually increased his work at the magazine to a full-time job.

"The cast of characters in those early days was as shifty as the characters in a floating poker game," White recalled. "People drifted in and drifted out. Every week the magazine teetered on the edge of financial ruin. It was chaos, but it was enjoyable."

MARRYING AN ANGELL

In 1929, White's first two books for adults were published. That same year—November 13— White married a young divorcee and editor of the *New Yorker,* Katharine Angell. Angell had two children from her first marriage.

"I soon realized I had made no mistake in my choice of a wife," he said. "I was helping her pack an overnight bag one afternoon when she said, 'Put in some tooth twine.' I knew then that a girl who called dental floss tooth twine was the girl for me. It had been a long search, but it was worth it." White's first son, Joel, was born on December 21, 1930.

In 1936 White was offered the editorship of the *Saturday Review of Literature,* but he declined the job. "I can't edit the *Saturday Review,* and this is the more painful for me because I like it," he said at the time. "At the *New Yorker,* I am an office boy deluxe—a happy and profitable arrangement. My function is solely contributive except for one or two perfunctory chores which I can now do with my left hind foot.

"I am appalled when I think of taking over the Review," he added. "My health is always whimsical, and I turn out shockingly little work in the course of a week—much less than I wish I did and far less than you imagine. Being the head of anything would bust me up in no time." What White wanted to do was write books full-time.

STUART LITTLE

In 1938 White took the first steps to further his book writing career. He moved to a farm in North Brooklyn, Maine. White maintained close ties with the *New Yorker.* He also contributed a monthly column, "One Man's Meat" to *Harper's* magazine. Then his book of poems, *The Fox of Peapack,* was published.

In 1939 White began writing his first children's book, *Stuart Little.* The principal character in the story had the attributes and appearance of a mouse.

The character of Stuart Little appeared to White in a dream. He came "all complete, with his hat, his cane, and his brisk manner," said White. "Since he was the only fractional figure ever to honor and disturb my sleep, I was deeply touched, and felt that I was not free to change him into a grasshopper or a wallaby. Luckily he bears no resemblance, either physically or temperamentally, to Mickey (Mouse). I guess that's a break for all of us."

In 1941 during World War II, the Whites returned to New York from Maine. Because many people were enlisting in the armed services, the *New Yorker* editorial staff had been drastically reduced. By 1943 White was back in Maine. He quit his monthly column for *Harper's* because he had difficulty writing the essays. They did not come naturally to him. "I have to go through the devil to get them written," he admitted.

In 1945 *Stuart Little* was finally published. It was illustrated by Garth Williams. White wrote the book with an unusual ending.

"Quite a number of children have written me to ask about Stuart," White said. "They want to know whether he got back home and whether he found Margalo. They are good questions but I did not answer them in the book because, in a way, Stuart's journey symbolizes the continuing journey that everybody takes—in search of what is perfect and unattainable. This is perhaps too elusive an idea to put into a book for children, but I put it in anyway."

In 1948 White received an honorary Doctor of Letters from Dartmouth College. The president of the college cited him for "literary bravery."

CHARLOTTE'S WEB

In 1952 *Charlotte's Web,* illustrated by Garth Williams, was published. The book—like all of White's juvenile books—was written on his

Maine farm. The story focuses on Wilbur, an insecure, vulnerable pig. Wilbur is saved from slaughter through the efforts of his barnyard friends—especially Charlotte, an ingenious and heroic spider. Charlotte spins the words "some pig," "terrific," "radiant," and "humble" into her web.

With Charlotte's help, Wilbur achieves both fame and maturity, understanding the meaning of true friendship as well as the place of death in the grand scheme of life.

White was inspired to write *Charlotte's Web* as he observed animals on his farm. "I like animals and my barn is a very pleasant place to be, at all hours," he said. "One day when I was on my way to feed the pig, I began feeling sorry for the pig because, like most pigs, he was doomed to die. This made me sad. So I started thinking of ways to save a pig's life. I had been watching a big, gray spider at her work and was impressed by how clever she was at weaving. Gradually I worked the spider into the story . . . a story of friendship and salvation on a farm."

Three years after he started writing his story, it was published. When illustrator Garth Williams tried to draw a spider that had human characteristics, the results were disastrous. He tried and tried, but he ended up with a Charlotte that was, as White described, "practically right out of a natural history book."

White pulled no punches in the story. The spider was not beautified in any way. But White did give her unusual abilities.

When asked the difference between writing for children and writing for adults, White responded: ". . . In my experience, the only difference (save for a very slight modification of vocabulary) is in one's state of mind. Children are a wonderful audience—they are so eager, so receptive, so quick. I have great respect for their powers of observation and reasoning. But like any good writer, I write to amuse myself, not some imaginary audience, and I rather suspect that it is a great help if one has managed never really to grow up.

"Some writers, I have noticed, have a tendency to write down to children," he added. "That way lies disaster. Other writers feel they must use only the easy words, the familiar words. I use any word I feel like using, on the theory that children enjoy new encounters and that I don't gain anything by depriving myself of the full scope of the language."

In 1958 *Charlotte's Web* received a Lewis Carroll Shelf Award as a book, the award committee said, was "worthy enough to sit on the shelf with *Alice in Wonderland*."

THE MEDAL OF FREEDOM

During 1963 White was named by President John F. Kennedy as one of thirty-eight Americans to receive the Presidential Medal of Freedom—the highest honor a civilian can receive in time of peace.

The late president of the United States, John F. Kennedy.

"I know President Kennedy must have approached the freedom award list as he approached everything else—with personal concern, lively interest, and knowledge," White said. "To find myself on his list was the most gratifying thing that ever happened to me, as well as a matter of pride and sober resolve."

THE TV EXPERIENCE

In 1966 *Stuart Little* was rewritten for television. White wasn't satisfied with the TV version, but he didn't expect to be. The program came out about the way he figured it would.

White's contract with NBC said that he could see and approve the script. In 1965 NBC sent him a script. White edited and returned the script with his approval. Weeks later, NBC told him they had lost or misplaced his copy with his revisions. Months later, a brand-new script arrived—with news that the entire project was finished. White never bothered to read it.

"It is the fixed purpose of television and motion pictures to scrap the author, sink him without a trace, on the theory that he is incompetent, has never read his own stuff, is not responsible for anything he ever wrote, and wouldn't know what to do about it even if he were," White said. "I believe this has something to do with the urge to create, and the only way a TV person or a movie person can become a creator is to sink the guy who did it to begin with."

White said he was not complaining about NBC because they set out to be faithful to the general theme of *Stuart Little*. They did not try to ruin the story. But there were "a hundred places" that he could have made it better for them.

Johnny Carson, a popular TV host, narrated the story. White liked those parts but felt Carson didn't read certain words right. The music was good, thought White—but overpowered and overrode the words. "The music," said White, "fought with the words just when it should have been peaceable."

TV talk show host, Johnny Carson, was the narrator of the TV version of *Stuart Little*.

SWAN SONG

In 1969 White worked on his third children's book, *The Trumpet of the Swan*. The seventy-year-old author worked three or four hours every morning, trying to finish it. By December 1969, the manuscript was sent to his publishers. White was greatly disappointed when he learned that Garth Williams had been turned down as the illustrator. He wrote to Williams: "I had always hoped that Williams and White would be as indestructible as ham and eggs, Scotch and soda, and [song writers] Gilbert and Sullivan."

In the years that followed, White was honored with more awards. In 1970 he received the Laura Ingalls Wilder Award for *Charlotte's Web* and *Stuart Little*. In 1971 he received the National Medal for Literature.

"I fell in love with the sound of an early typewriter and have been stuck with it ever since," he said. "I believed then, as I do now, in the goodness of the published word; it seemed to contain an essential goodness, like the smell of leaf mold. Being a medalist at last, I can now speak of the 'corpus' of my work—the word has a splendid sound. But glancing at the skimpy accomplishment of recent years, I find the 'cadaver of my work' a more fitting phrase."

TRAGEDY

In 1975 tragedy nearly struck the White household. Katharine White suffered a heart attack and almost died. The episode shook White's tranquil world. When Katharine returned home from the hospital to recover, he wrote to her: "This made me realize more than anything else ever has how much I love you and how little life would mean to me were you not here. Welcome back, and do not ever leave me."

In 1976 White celebrated the publication of *The Letters of E. B. White*. The book made White's birthday a well-known date.   But in 1977, what White feared the most finally happened. Katharine died, leaving him depressed and lonely.

The last year of White's life was a sad one. He had been at the shore one day, swimming or canoeing with a friend, when he fell. Two weeks later, he began to deteriorate. He became housebound, then bedridden.

E. B. White died on October 1, 1985. The cause of death was reported to be from Alzheimer's disease. But close friends say he died of a broken heart.

HIS MEMORY LIVES ON

Although E. B. White died in the mid 1980s, he still influences today's readers and writers. Six books of his essays remain in print. *The Elements of Style* has sold over a hundred thousand copies annually since it was published in 1959. It remains the essential manual for American writers.

But it is his three children's books that keep his memory bright. Each year, thousands of young readers discover *Stuart Little* and *The Trumpet of the Swan*. As for *Charlotte's Web*, it has been translated into fourteen languages. And it remains a world classic, easily holding its place among the most popular juvenile books in the United States and England.

E.B. White, author of the children classics
Charlotte's Web and *Stuart Little*.